Little Birthday Wishes

# Little Birthday Wishes

Illustrated by Becky Kelly

Written by Patrick Regan

**Andrews McMeel
Publishing**

Kansas City

ISBN: 0-7407-2088-0


02 03 04 05 06 LPP 10 9 8 7 6 5 4 3 2 1


*Illustrations by Becky Kelly*

*Design by Stephanie Farley*

*Edited by Jean Lowe*

*Production by Elizabeth Nuelle*

It seems that birthday wishes
have a way of coming true
so I am sending up some little wishes
to rain
down
on you.

I wish you clear eyes
and an open heart

to better take in
all the beauty that surrounds you.

I wish you a soul that is light,
a spirit that soars,

and a mind alive with
private dreams and powerful ideas.

I wish you the companionship
of those you love most,

And the pleasure
of your own company
in those times
you'd rather be alone.

I wish for you golden memories
of cherished moments,

whose luster only increases
with the passing of time;

And I hope that memories
of this birthday
will fit snugly into
your box of treasured recollections.

I wish for you
fresh-picked berries,
warm soothing tea,
and your favorite dessert
(for breakfast if you like!)

I wish you carefree giggles with friends,
familiar hands to hold,
and a sense of belonging
no matter where you are.

B. Kelly

I wish for you pleasant surprises,

Both slight and grand,

And the never-ending ability
to find true joy in life's little gifts.

And as you grow older,
I wish for you the continued ability
to focus on the growing
rather than the older.

I wish for you the peace
that comes from believing in yourself

and the joy to be found
in doing for others.

B. Kelly

And I truly hope you realize
the love that so many feel for you.

And as all these wishes fall softly
around your feet,

I'll add just one more wish:

That all of your
fondest birthday wishes
will come true.